Frogs

WONDER STARTERS

Frogs

Illustrated by Isobel Beard

Published by WONDER BOOKS
A Division of Grosset & Dunlap, Inc.
A Filmways Company

51 Madison Avenue   New York, N.Y. 10010

About Wonder Starters

Wonder Starters are vocabulary controlled information books for young children. More than ninety per cent of the words in the text will be in the reading vocabulary of the vast majority of young readers. Word and sentence length have also been carefully controlled.

Key new words associated with the topic of each book are repeated with picture explanations in the Starters dictionary at the end. The dictionary can also be used as an index for teaching children to look things up.

Teachers and experts have been consulted on the content and accuracy of the books.

Published in the United States by Wonder Books, a Division of Grosset & Dunlap, Inc.

Library of Congress Catalog Card Number: 76-50364
ISBN: 0-448-09690-0 (Trade Edition)
ISBN: 0-448-06448-0 (Library Edition)

First U.S. Printing 1977

© Macdonald and Company (Publishers),
Limited, 1971, London.

Printed and bound in the United States of America.

Frogs live near water.
They swim in the water.
They can swim well.

1

Frogs can stay on land too.
They stay where it is damp.
2

Frogs jump well.
They have long back legs.
Their long legs help them to jump.

The female frog is bigger
than the male frog.
The male frog croaks.
4

In spring the mother frog
lays some eggs in the pond.
The eggs are in jelly.
The jelly keeps the eggs safe.

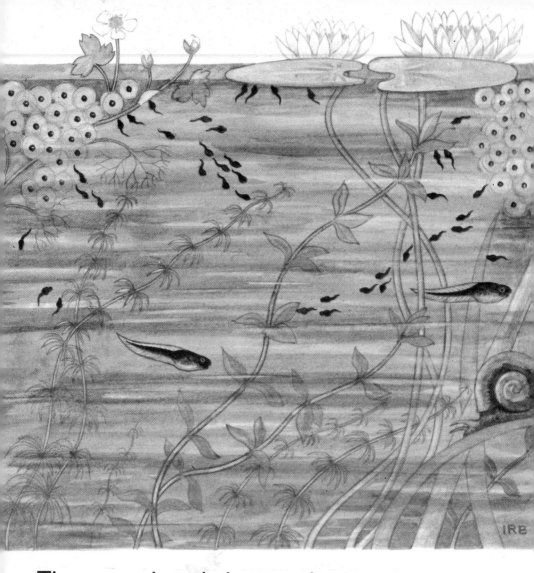

The eggs hatch into tadpoles.
The tadpole has a big head
and a long tail.
At first it eats plants.

6

The tadpole grows two back legs.
Then it grows two front legs.

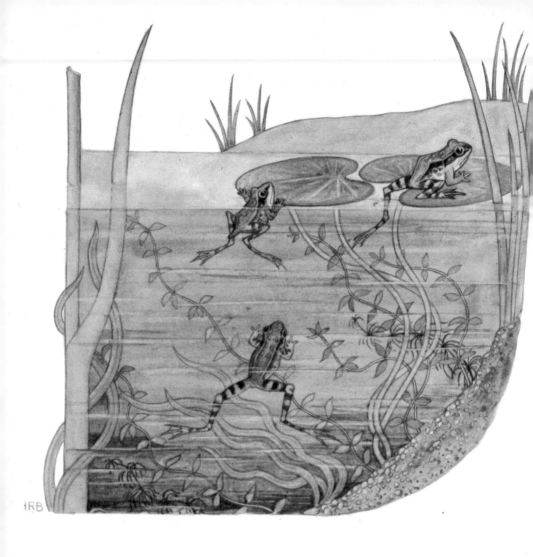

As it grows it changes shape.
It loses its tail.
Now the tadpole
has turned into a little frog.
8

The little frog gets bigger and bigger.
Its skin splits.
There is a new skin under the old one.
The frog pulls off the old skin and eats it.

9

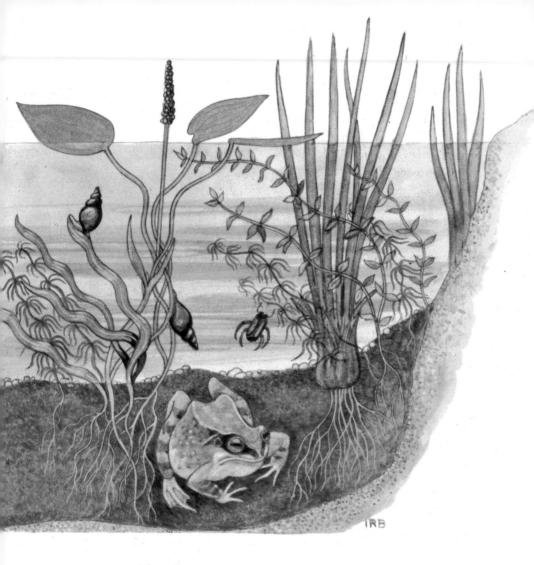

In winter the frog sleeps.
It sleeps in the mud in the pond.
It does not eat.
It breathes through its skin.

10

In spring it is warm again.
The frog wakes up.
The frog looks for food.

butterfly

ladybird

beetle

worm

snail

slug

The frog eats small animals.
It also eats insects.

12

The frog has
a long sticky tongue.
The frog catches insects with its tongue.

smallest frog

giant frog

There are more than 2,000 kinds of frogs.
The giant frog is 40 centimeters
(about 16 inches) long.
The smallest frog is 1 centimeter
(about 4/10 inch) long.
14

Some frogs live in trees.
Tree frogs have suckers on their toes.
The suckers help them climb trees.

Some tree frogs can change color.
When one sits on a leaf it is green.
When it sits on a branch it is brown.
It changes color so it won't be seen.
16

Some frogs can jump a very long way.
They are called flying frogs.
They do not really fly.
They just jump.

This frog is called an edible frog.
It is croaking.
18

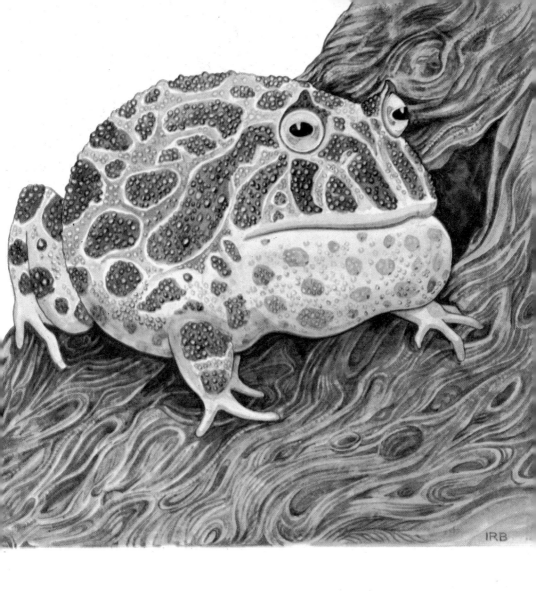

This frog has two bumps over its eyes.
They look like horns.
It is called the horned frog.

19

Some frogs have poison on their skin.
The poison keeps other animals away.

20

hawk

heron

stoat

snake

hedgehog

duck

fox

Some animals catch frogs to eat.
Some birds eat frogs too.

See for yourself.

In spring look for some frogs' eggs.
Keep them in some pond water.
Watch the eggs hatch into tadpoles.
The tadpoles will turn into frogs.

Starter's **Frogs** words

back legs
(page 3)

eggs
(page 5)

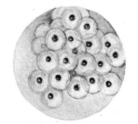

pond
(page 5)

tadpole
(page 6)

plant
(page 6)

butterfly
(page 12)

worm
(page 12)

beetle
(page 12)

snail
(page 12)

tongue
(page 13)

tree frog
(page 15)

flying frog
(page 17)

suckers
(page 15)

edible frog
(page 18)

toes
(page 15)

horned frog
(page 19)

leaf
(page 16)

hedgehog
(page 21)

branch
(page 16)

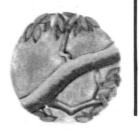

heron
(page 21)